When You Have to Say Goodbye
Loving and Letting Go of Your Pet

Written by Monica Mansfield, D.V. M.
Illustrated by Lennie Peterson

Copyright © 2011 Monica Mansfield
Illustrations copyright © 2011 Lennie Peterson

Beanpole Books
PO Box 242 - Midway, FL 32343

First Edition
ISBN 13: 978-0-9831032-1-9

CPSIA facility code: BP 313326

This book was inspired by Second Lieutenant Ian Thomas McVey.

Sometimes a pet is lucky enough to be loved by you. After all, kids know how to love animals in an extra special way.

When you love an animal and the animal loves you, there is a deep understanding between the two of you.

Your pet is always
happy to see you.

She never uses angry
words.

She listens to all
of your secrets.

Cats turn on their purr motors and dogs
wag their tails.

Pets are funny, they are sweet, and they always love you back.

When you feel cheerful, they are cheerful too.

When you need a hug, they are by your side.

Sometimes pets are a great comfort when you miss somebody.

If your pet becomes sick or hurt, you might feel sad or scared.

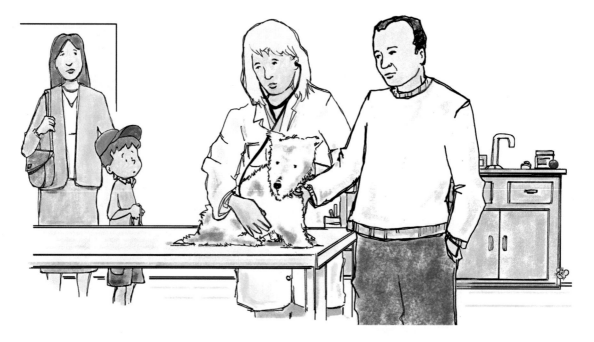

Your family may need to bring your pet to the veterinarian, who is a special doctor just for animals. The veterinarian will try to find out what is wrong.

Most of the time there are medicines or treatments that can help animals feel much better.

Usually, your pet will improve quickly.

But sometimes there is no way to cure an illness.

Sometimes when an animal is very sick, very old, or badly hurt, it might be time for her life to end. That happens to every living creature.

An animal's life is much shorter than a human's life.

That just doesn't seem fair, does it?

This is the hardest part about loving a pet.

When a pet is sick, it is hard for her to understand why she feels different.

Perhaps her bones make it too painful to walk easily.

Or it might be too difficult for her to go to the bathroom the right way.

There are diseases, like cancer or kidney failure, that can keep some of the inside body parts from doing their job.

Maybe there has been a bad accident and she has been terribly hurt.

If your pet's body is having a lot of trouble, there may be a day when there is nothing else the veterinarian can do to make your pet feel better. Your family might need to make a very difficult decision with the veterinarian's help.

When this day comes, the veterinarian will give your pet a special medicine that will help her die peacefully and quickly so she will no longer feel bad or feel pain.

It will be the kindest and most loving thing to do.

This is called euthanasia. It doesn't hurt the animal and will help her die gently.

If the day comes that you have to say goodbye to your pet, it will be very sad for everyone. It will be okay for you to cry.

Your mom and dad might cry too. Some kids feel better if their parents put their arms around them and hold on tight.

Some kids prefer to be
by themselves.

Some kids even
feel angry.

Whatever you may feel, it is okay.

It's okay to be sad for a long time, but it's important that you talk about it with someone who knows you and cares about you.

You can talk to your mom or dad, your teacher, your grandparent, your brother or sister, your friend, your friend's mom or dad, or someone else you trust.

There will be a person you know who understands exactly how you feel.

There are some things you can do to feel better. Some kids find it helpful to write a poem. You might try that.

Or you can draw a cartoon about your adventures with your pet. You can write in a journal or notebook.

You can look at photos of your animal.

You can write a letter to your pet or draw a big picture of her and frame it.

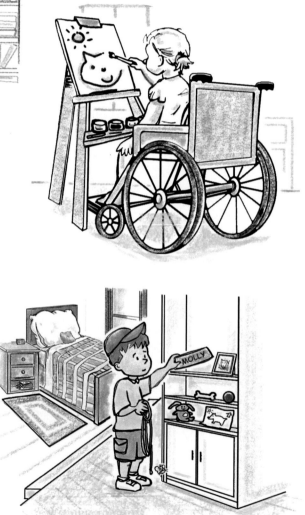

You can make a special place with a few of her favorite toys or her collar.

Your parents can help you plant a flower or a bush in the yard in her memory.

You can tell funny stories about some of the naughty or silly or lovely things your pet did.

After a while, the part of you that feels bad when your pet dies won't hurt so much.

Eventually the hurting part will be replaced with a tender spot that sits like a soft pillow in your heart.

If you have been lucky enough to love a pet, you
have known a great gift.

You will remember your friend for the rest of your life.

The reason you feel so sad when your pet dies is that your heart felt a lot of love when your pet was alive. The love will be with you forever.

The love is the greatest part.

(place photo
or drawing
of pet here)